BUILDING BLOCKS OF ENGLISH

ADVANCED CONSONANTS AND VOWELS

Written by Jeff De La Rosa

Illustrated by Ruth Bennett

WORLD BOOK

a Scott Fetzer company
Chicago

Co-published by agreement between Shi Tu Hui and World Book, Inc.

Shi Tu Hui
Room 1807, Block 1,
#3 West Dawang Road
Chaoyang District, Beijing 100025
P.R. China

World Book, Inc.
180 North LaSalle Street
Suite 900
Chicago, Illinois 60601
USA

WORLD BOOK STAFF

Editorial

Vice President
Tom Evans

Senior Manager, New Content
Jeff De La Rosa

Curriculum Designer
Caroline Davidson

Proofreader
Nathalie Strassheim

Graphics and Design

Senior Visual Communications Designer
Melanie Bender

Library of Congress Control Number: 2024936272

Building Blocks of English
ISBN: 978-0-7166-5517-6 (set, hardcover)

Advanced Consonants and Vowels
ISBN: 978-0-7166-5519-0 (hardcover)

Also available as:
ISBN: 978-0-7166-5529-9 (e-book)
ISBN: 978-0-7166-5539-8 (soft cover)

Acknowledgments:
Writer: Jeff De La Rosa
Illustrator: Ruth Bennett/The Bright Agency
Series Advisor: Marjorie Frank

TABLE OF CONTENTS

There is a glossary on page 40. Terms defined in the glossary
are in type **that looks like this** on their first appearance.

There, he met King K and his consonant court.

...and return to the land of the vowels.

Y needed a plan to stop a war between the consonants and vowels.

He gathered S, T, O, and P together. He used them to spell out the word STOP.

5

You have taught us to work together.

But why, Y? Why do you care if consonants and vowels get along?

Because I am both consonant and vowel!

GASP!

It's true. I act as a consonant when I start a word...

...as in YARD and YAK.

Other times, I act as a vowel...

...as in FLY and DRY.

The letter O is my mother...

That is why I rescued her.

I came to your kingdom in search of my father...

...the mysterious letter X.

Is Y a consonant or vowel in the word CRY? YEAR? YOU? See page 40 for answers.

7

9

BOAT
But what about this in the middle?
Two vowels, but only one sound?
That is called a **vowel team...**
...two vowels working together to make a single sound.
In this case, O and A team up...
...to make a long O sound.

CONSONANT BLENDS

Good work, young Y. We've made it this far!

But, I am confused by this next set of clues.

Vowel teams do not seem to fit here.

CLI__ into the hills.

Go past the big __EE.

Turn left at the FO__ in the road.

Aha! You vowels are not the only ones that can work together.

CONSONANT DIGRAPHS

MB is not a blend, at all.

It's a different kind of consonant team, called a **consonant digraph.**

In a digraph, two consonants combine...

...to form a new sound!

POOF!

M and B form an M sound...

BUZZ

BUZZ

...with perhaps a little extra hum.

Heh, you never know when you're going to need the right word!

This island is full of wild donkeys.

Maybe we could use them to carry the words.

That will work for short words.

But, longer words are too heavy for these poor animals.

STAR

FLOWER

A word can have any number of syllables.

The word SYLLABLE has three!

Now you are getting it!

So, a one syllable word, like JUMP, will fit on one donkey.

FLOWER has two syllables...

We can put FLOW- on one donkey...

...and -ER on another!

JUMP

FLOW

ER

I put BANANA on three donkeys!

How many donkeys will be needed to carry each word?
(Remember, that's one donkey per syllable!)
See page 40 for answers.

Later...

We must be on the right path.

Your father's mark!

It is more beautiful than I imagined!

THE SILENT E
The silent E is a relic of our people!
Added to the end of a syllable...
It turns a **short vowel** into a **long vowel.**

It turns FIN into FINE...
...and HOP into HOPE.

I present it to you, O...

...and to all the vowels.

Which of these words have a long vowel sound: FAT, FATE, RIP, RIPE? See page 40 for answers.

What a wonderful gift!

I give you my blessing to live in peace.

I give you my blessing, too.

And they lived happily ever after.

37

SHOW WHAT YOU KNOW

1. Which of these words contain vowel teams?

SPENT
COAL
SAIL
EXIT
CHIP
CREEK

2. Which of these words contain consonant blends? Which contain consonant digraphs?

PARK
WITH
SHOE
TRIP
POST
COUGH

3. How many syllables do each of these words have?

HAPPY
FISH
PURPLE
UMBRELLA
DOOR

4. Identify the silent letter in the following words:

ALIGN
FATE
KNOT
WRIST

See page 40 for answers.

ANSWERS

page 7: CRY- VOWEL
YEAR- CONSONANT
YOU- CONSONANT

page 13: Sail into the BAY.
Land on the BEACH here.
Watch out for the SNAIL!

page 21: Vowel teams: AI, OU
Consonant blends: PR, ST
Digraphs: CH, TH

page 28: GRASS-1
MONKEY-2
NOODLE-2
MOON-1
ELEPHANT-3

page 33: CASTLE
KNOT
TWO

page 37: FATE
RIPE

SHOW WHAT YOU KNOW ANSWERS
pages 38-39:

1. COAL, SAIL, CREEK

2. consonant blends: PARK, TRIP, POST
consonant digraphs: WITH, SHOE,
COUGH

3. HAPPY- 2
FISH- 1
PURPLE- 2
UMBRELLA- 3
DOOR- 1

4. ALIGN
FATE
KNOT
WRIST

WORDS TO KNOW

consonant a letter sounded by stopping or slowing the breath with tongue, teeth, or lips

consonant blend a consonant team in which both consonants lend their sound

consonant digraph a consonant team in which the consonants combine to form a new sound

long vowel a vowel whose sound matches its spoken name

short vowel a vowel whose sound does not match its spoken name

silent E an unpronounced E that turns a vowel long when added to the end of a syllable

silent letter a letter in a spelled word that is not pronounced

syllable a word or part of a word pronounced as a single unit

vowel a letter with an open sound, in which the breath flows freely

vowel team multiple vowels working together to make a single sound

www.ingramcontent.com/pod-product-compliance
Lightning Source LLC
Chambersburg PA
CBHW060858090426
42737CB00023B/3487